Heart to Heart

Heart to Heart

NERRISA LU

StoryTerrace

Text Nerrisa Lu
Copyright © Nerrisa Lu

First print January 2025

www.StoryTerrace.com

For the heart warriors that have lost the fight or are still fighting. For Bri-bird who fights the good fight alongside me. Together, we are immortal through memories.

CONTENTS

MY FATHER'S DAUGHTER — 9

1. THE INVISIBLE DISABILITY — 15

2. THE PHYSICAL PAIN — 23

3. ABOUT FAITH — 33

4. THE SUPPORT SYSTEM — 45

5. FYI — 59

6. ABOUT RECOVERY — 67

7. WHAT NOW? — 75

8. YOUR HOMEWORK — 79

9. MY LAST WORDS — 85

THANK YOU — 89

MY FATHER'S DAUGHTER

As a heart transplant recipient, I've spent more time in medical facilities than most people ever will. But hospitals have always felt like a second home to me, even long before my transplant journey began. My mother passed away from cardiac arrest when I was barely a year old. The same month I celebrated my first birthday, my father became a widower and single parent. It wasn't until much later that I learned of my mother's condition—a mutated gene that leads to hypertrophic cardiomyopathy (HCM), which causes the heart muscle to become abnormally thick. That same faulty gene had been passed down to me.

Did you know that you can make a designer baby now by taking the mutated genes out of your egg? What kind of sorcery is that? Amazing! Anyways, you are probably not surprised with the technology advancement because of what you've already gone through or about to go through.

As a kid, I didn't fully grasp the severity of my congenital heart condition. I was blissfully living my childhood to the fullest. My father nurtured my adventurous spirit and celebrated my fearlessness. My father has been my only parent, which means he is the person I go to for everything! He gives the best advice and the most comfort a scared child or now, a very grown adult, would need. He is the center of my life.

HEART TO HEART

One of my most cherished core memories is of long car rides with my father, just the two of us, singing at the top of our lungs. Our favorite song was a duet called 'Don't Cry Joni' by Conway Twitty and his daughter Joni Lee. I didn't understand a word of English at the time, but I'd belt it out with gusto, matching my father's enthusiasm if not his pronunciation.

Those car rides often took us high into the mountains of Taiwan. I don't remember where we were going, but when we took long rides with just him and I, it was usually to see my mom. Her resting place isn't the easiest to get to and I am not sure if I can get to it now without him. When I was little, I just assumed this was something that we would always be doing together, forever. It was something that was just for us.

Other moments that would also become "our thing" were going to the hospital, emergency room (ER), and intensive care unit (ICU). My heart condition was not the only health concern Dad and I had. As a kid, my school would call my dad to come get me because I was having an asthma attack. I also had allergies that required me to get weekly shots. When we were in the hospital, I would request to go to the maternity floor to look at newborn babies through the nursery window while I waited for my appointment. There was something comforting and fun in watching tiny infants.

Growing up, it wasn't just me and my dad—I also had my sister. While my father was my protector and cheerleader, my sister was my confidant and partner in crime. We shared a room, and I loved showing off my daredevil antics to her. I'd proudly demonstrate how I could climb onto a shelf and hide in our room and then leap off onto my bed. I felt like a spider monkey, agile and fearless. Spider monkey is what I was! We had bunk beds that were not directly on top of each other, but mine was still attached to hers at a higher level. She watched with admiration and excitement when I'd climb up and jump off, flying to the top of my bed. We were both small at the time but she was even smaller. To two little girls, climbing the bookshelf at that time felt like climbing the Empire State Building! I wanted my sister to admire me because she was the only person at the time who made me feel special. My dad was very busy traveling internationally for work. Sisters are your best secret keepers, if you don't have one I feel sorry for you.

At 11 years old, I walked into sixth grade as a foreigner where I understood maybe 50% of what was being said around me. The school hallways felt like a United Colors of Benetton ad come to life—a blurred memory of a mix of faces and accents that left me disoriented.

I can still vividly recall that day. The shouts of "Fight! Fight! Fight!" as a crowd gathered. There was a girl in my face calling me different items listed on a Chinese restaurant menu. "Egg rolls" and "Compow chicken." Now that I am very familiar with English, I learned that what the girl was doing was called "popping off" and what I should've done was use words like "Come at me bi-otch!" Instead, my fists did the talking. Never mess with a girl who's only way of communication is with actions. The incident was over quickly —I may have been smaller, but I left her with a bloody nose and a healthy dose of humiliation. Of course, I was the one who threw the first punch, so I ended up suspended while she got off with a warning. Leaving school, I thought that I would be in huge trouble. The phone call with my dad was not what I had expected. He wasn't angry at all—he was proud of me for standing up for myself. He knew the importance of being able to advocate for yourself in a world that isn't always kind.

His words filled me with a warmth that went beyond pride. It was a reminder that in his eyes, I've never been defined by my illness or limited by my health challenges. To him, I'm not a fragile patient or a medical miracle—I'm just his daughter, capable of anything I set my mind to.

My dad's influence goes beyond just emotional support. His approach to life—his optimism, his resilience, his ability to find joy in small moments—has profoundly shaped my own outlook. Even in the darkest times, when my health was at its worst and the future looked bleak, he never lost hope. And because of that, neither did I. He is my rock, my champion, my inspiration. I am, in every sense, my father's daughter.

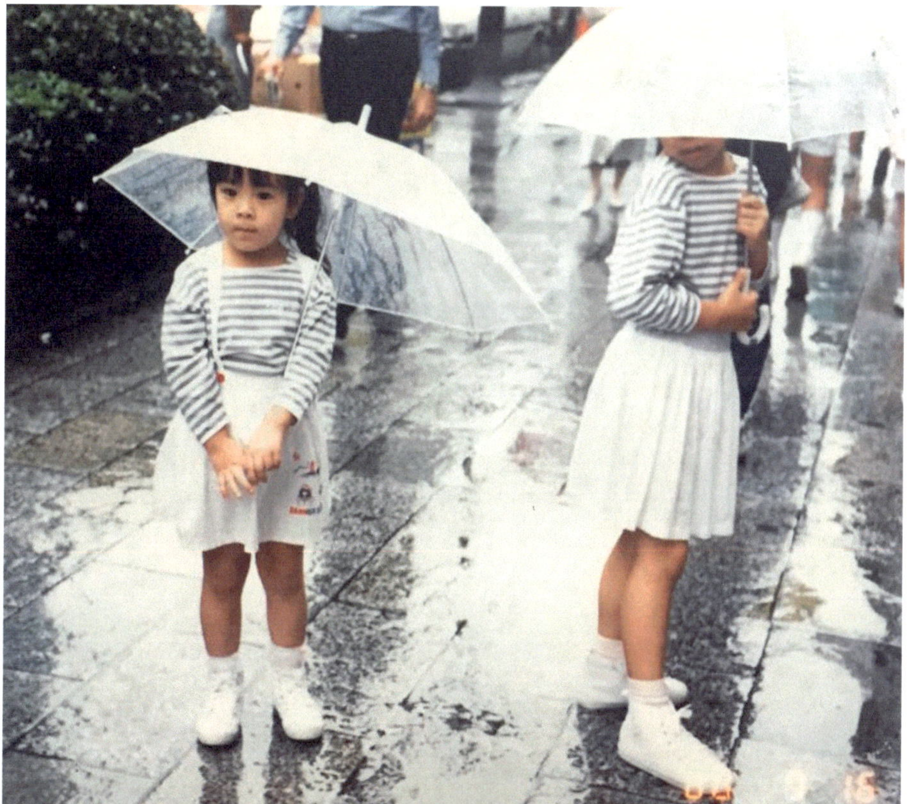

LIGHT
travel
FASTER
than sound

1. THE INVISIBLE DISABILITY

"*Light travels faster than sound.*" "*You see us, but you need to hear us.*"— Unknown

Light travels faster than sound. As a heart transplant recipient, this phrase has taken on new meaning in my life. People see me before they hear my story. Their eyes take in my appearance—a seemingly healthy, active woman—but can they process the reality of my invisible disability?

You don't believe something until you can witness it with your own eyes. This has become how we make judgments, by the cover, which I hope was one of the reasons why you purchased this book. Don't worry, the inside is quite pretty too. We need to learn that just because you can't see it, doesn't mean it's not there. What's that saying? "If a tree falls in a forest and no one is around, does it make a sound?" The answer is YES. We still hurt and we are still in pain, whether anyone sees it or not. Most of the time, we are hiding that pain from the public and from others to make everyone feel comfortable, maybe less awkward.

One of the best things that comes with a disability is a DISABILITY PLACARD! If you live in a city that is expensive and hilly and hard to find parking, you would understand what a gold mine it is to have a handicap placard. San Francisco, my home, is notorious for its steep hills and limited parking. There are days I considered not leaving my house because I dreaded the walk. With the benefits of a handicap placard, you can park in a spot longer than the maximum of two hours, which gives me time to slowly crawl up these hills at the speed of a snail. Sometimes I see snails passing me—I am not joking.

The placard is a lifesaver, but it comes with its own set of challenges. It's like a visible symbol of an invisible condition, and people often feel entitled to question its validity. I have been stopped by cops several times asking me if the placard was mine, which is OK because I take it as a compliment and the cops are only doing their job. Other than cops, I've also been stopped by meter maids, "Karens," and just people that have nothing better to do.

One night while parking my car at a handicap spot, a man actually told me that I looked too pretty to be handicapped. I replied, "Are handicapped people supposed to be ugly?" That was enough to make the man turn the other way. I got this reply, "YOU LOOK TOO HEALTHY TO BE HANDICAPPED!" I just thanked him. These interactions, while sometimes frustrating, are a reminder of disability assumptions.

Having a disability that is not visible also lets me become a pathological liar—and what others perceive as a very boring person. There are so many lies that I have come up with over the years that helped me to get out of physical activities that I cannot do. When I moved to San Francisco, I was determined to create a life not defined by my illness. Quickly, I learned that my heart condition made me different from my peers and coworkers in ways I wanted to conceal.

If coworkers or friends asked, "Want to get together for a hike?" my response was, "I do not like nature, and I am lazy." If my employer asked, "Let's tour the company factory?" my response was, "I am sad to miss out but I have a prior commitment that day." I was starting to get used to people at my company calling me "princess" or "lazy." I became skilled at making excuses to hide my physical limitations, like pretending to move my car to avoid walking hills. It was the easier choice to not reveal the real reason why a short walk felt like a marathon to me.

These lies, while protecting me in the short term, came with their own set of problems. Once I started to lie too much, it had risks of believing the lies myself. I found myself almost buying into the persona I had created—the lazy princess who didn't like nature. But deep down, I knew the truth. I love nature. I love being active. My body just couldn't keep up with my desires.

Knowing deep down that it is not true, I choose to go hiking alone, at my own pace, where no one can judge or rush me.

Family and close friends are beginning to understand my disability. "Uber? Seriously? It's only four blocks away!" Roll your eyes and forgive your friends when they have these comments. They do forget about your disability sometimes and need a reminder from time to time. Just remember, they do not know how you feel and never will. The next time they walk too fast or are aggravated you walk too slow, don't be offended and just remind them. My best advice is to tell them to walk ahead so you won't be pressured into going at another person's pace. You may not have a disabled "look" that can serve as a constant reminder to someone, but take that as a blessing.

My life took an unexpected turn when I was 30 years old. I had a stroke and the damage was to my right brain, which affected the left side of my body temporarily. I was so worried that my disability was no longer invisible. My first thought was that I had no way of blending in with the healthy people anymore. Luckily I was young, my brain rerouted around the damaged area, and the left side of my body started to function normally again after a short amount of time. Phew, that was a close call, I was almost visibly disabled.

Now I'd like to touch on the topic of dating, because dating and romance is a normal part of our lives. If it's not for you, yet, it should be! You deserve happiness and romance in your life. My dating experience was a big fat joke! I wish it were a six-foot, smart, and handsome joke! Dating in my 20s and 30s was especially sketchy. I was a big catfish whether you met me online or in person. My fake identity was a healthy young woman who is going to live until old age and can go on any adventure with you. As long as that adventure does not require traveling.

I've hidden medications and downplayed my health conditions in my relationships so my partners wouldn't see me as a burden. It is true, someone who truly loves you would stay. However, starting out a relationship is hard enough without the health drama. You also go through a lot of disappointment before finding your person—THE one.

I've had my share of heartbreak too (pun intended). I had a person that actually left me in the middle of a date because I walked too slowly. It started off as a coffee date where we both agreed to bring our dogs. He suggested a place near the beach. First, I had to pretend that I drank coffee, then after our coffee he suggested a walk on the beach. Worst-case scenario happened, yup, he left me in the middle of this walk on the beach and disappeared into the San Francisco fog. I was alone and mortified.

Living with an invisible disability is a constant process of educating others and advocating for yourself. It's about finding the balance between blending in and standing up for your needs. It's about learning to love yourself, limitations and all, and finding others who accept you for who you are.

So the next time you see someone who looks "too healthy" to be using a handicap placard, or someone who seems "lazy" for not joining in on physical activities, remember: light may travel faster than sound, but it's the sound—the stories, the experiences, the unseen struggles— that truly matter. You see us, but you need to hear us. Our disabilities may be invisible, but our voices don't have to be.

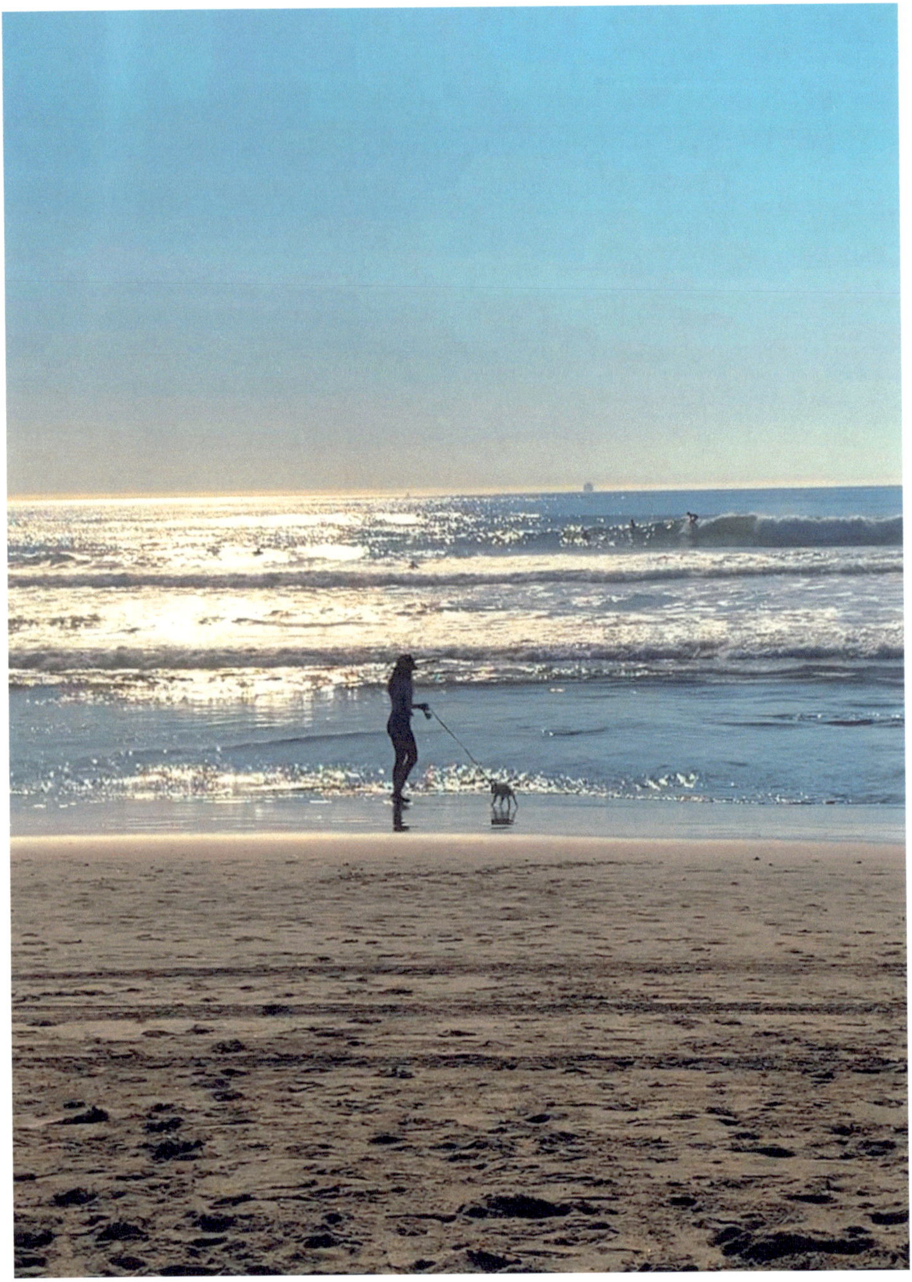

Where there is no struggle, there is no strength - Oprah

2. THE PHYSICAL PAIN

"*Where there is no struggle, there is no strength.*"— Oprah Winfrey

Before we dive into the nitty-gritty of my pre-transplant life, let me share a story that impacted me. Recently, I came across a YouTube video of Jensen Huang, the CEO of Nvidia, giving a talk at Stanford about building resilience through pain. His words hit home in a way I wasn't expecting.

Huang spoke about the importance of having low expectations. He argued that people with high expectations often have very low resilience. This concept fascinated me because, in my experience, living with a chronic heart condition forced me to constantly adjust my expectations. Huang went on to say that resilience is crucial for success and that greatness comes from character—character that is formed through suffering.

As I listened to Huang's words, I felt his insights on the role of resilience in success were truly enlightening. The struggles I faced with my heart condition, the pain I endured, and the challenges I overcame—all of these experiences shaped my character and built my resilience.

Now, let's talk about pain. And not just any pain—we're talking about the kind of pain that makes you question your existence, the kind that makes you wonder if it's worth fighting anymore. Having heart disease impacts your respiratory system, and breathing can be difficult, which causes extreme amounts of pain to your chest, and the rest of your body tightens up too. I know as a heart patient I don't have to tell you this. But for anyone who's not, it's important for them to know—it hurts! Hurts worse than a bitch-slap!

I learned from a young age to tolerate high amounts of pain caused by my body. I powered through the pain. I didn't want anything to hold me back from living life the way I wanted. By doing this, I created a much higher threshold or tolerance of pain than the average person.

Heart failure patients have an unbelievable level of pain tolerance. If anyone in this world has some kind of superhuman power, it is us. Doctors often ask if I experience any nausea or fatigue from a new treatment or medication. I give them a blank look as I have no idea how to answer that question. I am on more than five medications that have similar side effects. I think I wake up with nausea and fatigue, which is probably our normal. We are not afraid of needles and can often deal with the poke without taking any pain medications. If you ever have to take any diuretics, we also have the ability to hold our pee for a long time. We have trained our iron bladder. My girlfriends need a numbing cream or ice on their faces before receiving Botox. Eye-rolls. I've been injecting myself with blood thinners in my tummy! Girl, Botox is nothing.

HEART TO HEART

    This high pain tolerance became both a blessing and a curse. On one hand, it allowed me to push through challenges that might have stopped others in their tracks. On the other hand, it sometimes led me to ignore warning signs that I should have heeded. But we'll get to that later.

    First, let me tell you about my best friend, Amaya. She's a beautiful girl from the Ivory Coast who I often saw in the elevator going to our graduate-school classes. At first, I thought she was talking to herself, until I realized she had a wireless earbud—stylish, high-tech. We finally had a class together, and she seemed very desperate to be my friend. I later learned that she was a very spiritual and intuitive girl and that she knew early on we would be very good friends. How can you not want such a positive energy like her to be in your life?

    Amaya is my twin flame, we are soul sisters—or shall I say pain sisters. Amaya has lupus, and our journeys with chronic illness have ended up having so much in common, in an unusual way.

    Having Amaya in my life has been a blessing. She understands the struggles of living with an invisible illness in a way that most people can't. We've spent countless hours comparing notes on medications, side effects, and the general absurdity of navigating life with a chronic condition. She's the one I call when I'm having a bad day, and I'm the one she turns to when her lupus is flaring up. Our friendship is a testament to the strength that can be found in shared struggles. Who knew the hate for prednisone could connect two people so much? I have to admit Amaya is far stronger than me. She has to deal with daily pain and raise two children at the same time. She's lucky that she has an amazing husband and family to support her. I can never imagine having the responsibility of taking care of two children while going through an illness that lasts a lifetime.

Now, let's talk about AFib—atrial fibrillation. If you've never experienced it, consider yourself lucky. The first time I went into AFib, I thought my heart was going to explode—the pain and breathlessness were terrifying. It starts off with a numbing sensation and you know something is coming. When the numbness travels to your stomach from your toes, your stomach begins to hurt. You run to the bathroom thinking that you ate something wrong, then your other organs start to feel like they are twisting in your body. You become breathless, all you see is a white blur before you start to fall to the floor.

This began a cycle of ambulance rides, ER visits, medication adjustments, and short hospital stays every time my heart went into AFib. I became frustrated that my body kept betraying me and exposing my illness to the world, making it harder to maintain my "normal" exterior. I started to feel more resigned than shocked each time I landed in the back of an ambulance. The ambulance became like my angel, arriving to take me somewhere safe.

Each AFib episode was a stark reminder of the fragility of my health. It was a battle between my desire to live a normal life and the reality of my condition. I found myself constantly on edge, wondering when the next episode would hit. Would it be during a work meeting? In the middle of a date? While I was alone in my apartment? The unpredictability of it all was almost as challenging as the episodes themselves.

But perhaps the most insidious enemy I faced wasn't AFib or even my failing heart—it was stairs. What is the thing I fear the most? More than demons, monsters, serial killers? STAIRS! They are the devil himself, I am telling you! I hated the physical limitations that stairs and hills created for me.

Living in San Francisco, a city famous for its steep hills, was both a dream and a nightmare. The views were breathtaking, but so was the simple act of walking up the street to my apartment. I constantly felt the need to prove I was just as capable as everyone else, pushing my body to the brink to keep up appearances. I struggled with the disconnect between my healthy exterior and the pain and breathlessness I felt inside. I lived in fear of my secret being exposed, of being seen as weak or incapable.

There were days when I would stand at the bottom of a staircase, looking up at what seemed like an insurmountable obstacle. My heart would race just at the thought of climbing those steps. But I would take a deep breath, gather all my strength, and start the ascent. Each step was a battle, each landing a brief respite before the next challenge. By the time I reached the top, I would be breathless, my heart pounding so hard I thought it might burst out of my chest. But I made it. Every. Single. Time.

Even as my health deteriorated, I clung to a sense of pride and denial about the severity of my condition. I never let my heart condition stop me from trying new things or keeping up with my peers, even if it meant pushing my body harder than

I should. Each of these activities was a silent rebellion against my failing heart, a way of saying, "You don't control me."

But my body had other plans. As I approached my late 30s, my heart function began to decline more rapidly. The episodes of AFib became more frequent, the stairs became more daunting, and the facade of normalcy I had worked so hard to maintain began to crumble.

At 37, I hit a breaking point. My worsening heart function made me eligible for a transplant, but in a cruel twist of fate, I was denied from the organ donation waitlist. The reason? I was too healthy. Yes, you read that right. My years of pushing through the pain, of maintaining an active lifestyle despite my condition, had created a paradox. On paper, I looked healthier than I actually was.

This denial was a wake-up call. It forced me to confront the reality of my situation in a way I had been avoiding for years. I had to admit that despite my best efforts, my heart was failing. I had to acknowledge that my struggle, while it had made me strong in many ways, was also putting my life at risk.

In the weeks following this denial, I found myself reevaluating everything. I thought about all the times I had pushed my body to its limits, all the times I had ignored the warning signs, all the times I had chosen appearance over health. I realized that my strength, the very thing I had prided myself on, had become a double-edged sword.

The story doesn't end here. It's merely the prelude to a symphony of survival, an overture to an opus of resilience. The next movement awaits, with its own set of notes to master and rhythms to conquer. And as for me? I'm just warming up my heart for the grand performance to come.

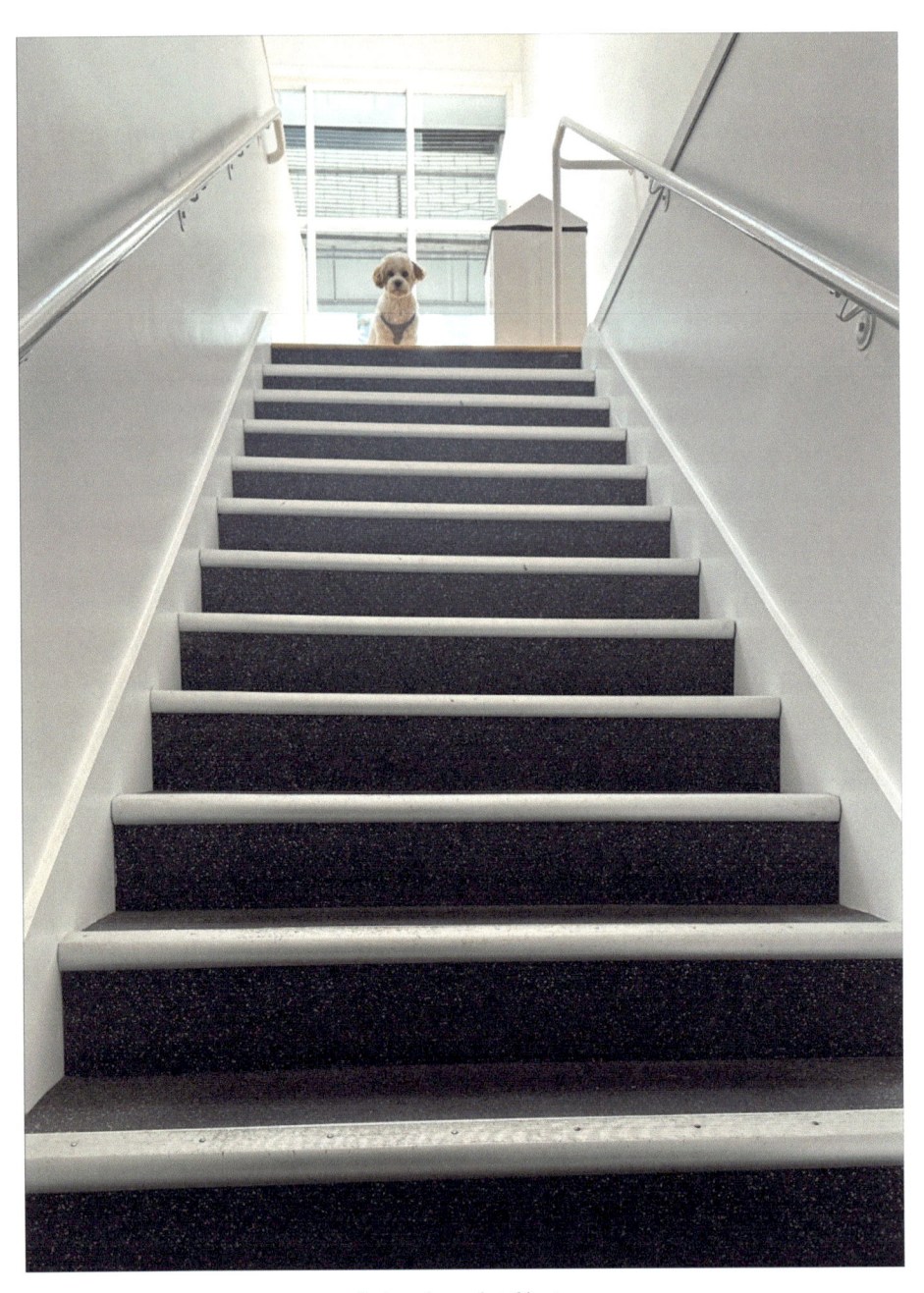

Stairs - the scariest thing to see

NEVER
give
UP AND
good luck
WILL FIND
you -
FALCOR

3. ABOUT FAITH

"*Never give up and good luck will find you.*"—Falkor, the Luck Dragon, *The Neverending Story,* by Michael Ende

When you're flying and the plane suddenly hits terrible turbulence, what goes through your mind? Do you pray to a higher power? Clutch a lucky charm? Hope for the best? At your most vulnerable, what gives you hope to feel safe?

Though I attended Jesuit schools my whole life, even college, I was never particularly religious. My Buddhist grandmother liked to sit in her chair, prayer beads in hand, play a repetitive hymn while reading a book and repeating after the tape—not connecting with what she was doing. I guess I would call myself spiritual. The day I found out I was to receive a new heart, I went to the place where I could gather the most amount of prayers in the shortest amount of time—Facebook.

"Hi friends, sorry that this is a post and not a personal message, this is very sudden news, even for me. I received a match this morning and am going into surgery to get a new heart tonight. I will have to explain later as I have no time to go into details. I need all hands on deck, please ask your family, friends, pets, exes, etc. to pray for me. Pray for anything you believe in, if you don't belong to any religion. I need all positive vibes and energy sent my way. My friend, Sandy, will keep you updated if or when I get out of surgery."—Facebook post on June 26th, 2020

But let's rewind to how I ended up in the hospital. As a hobby career, I'm a group fitness instructor. With my heart condition, I had to choose my workouts carefully. Reformer Pilates provided a good strengthening routine—high intensity but low impact. Modifications let you go at your own pace and limits.

The stronger your body, the less work for your heart. Before your transplant, it's crucial to build muscle. More leg muscle means less strain on your heart when walking or climbing stairs. It also speeds recovery, potentially letting you skip rehab post-transplant.

I got pretty good at Pilates and decided to become an instructor. After getting certified, I started teaching BODYROK Pilates two nights a week after my day job. Then COVID hit and I pivoted to teaching mat Pilates via Zoom. One morning mid-class, my breathing changed and heart rate spiked. The familiar feeling of AFib took over. I tried to act normal as seven people watched and listened through their screens. Usually this feeling would pass, but this time it only worsened.

I told the group to give me a few minutes as I struggled to breathe. Stumbling to the bathroom, I waited for my heart to find its rhythm again. Instead, the pain intensified. My body ached everywhere as I collapsed to the floor. Remembering my Zoom attendees, I crawled back to the computer. With my last breath, I told them I had to call an ambulance before shutting my laptop. My friend on Zoom freaked out and tried dialing 911 herself. My worst fear was coming true—scaring my clients as they watched me fall out of frame, wondering if I was dying before their eyes.

Through the pain, I summoned the strength to call 911. Barely able to speak, I explained that I was on the heart transplant waitlist. Curled up in a ball, my stomach and back seized with sharp, stabbing pains. I reached out to a higher power. "Please God take away this pain. I don't mind if you kill me now, just make it stop please." Then I reconsidered. "Wait God, actually I don't want to die, let me live but take this pain away. I promise to be a good person, I will give you my first child!"

The dispatcher stayed on the line until help arrived—an ambulance and fire truck with six burly men. In my bedroom, I grabbed my prepacked "hospital bag" containing essentials for the optimal hospital stay. One emergency medical technician (EMT) had me lie down to take my vitals and asked me questions. Everything blurred together. They brought up a stretcher and carried me out. As they wheeled me away, I remember saying, "Please make sure my dog doesn't run out and grab my luggage." Even in an emergency, I'm particular about the details.

Seeing my neighbors' terrified faces as I was taken to the ambulance, I was sure they assumed I had COVID. This was peak lockdown after all. In the ambulance, they cut open my shirt, ready to resuscitate me if needed. An EMT started an IV. So many thoughts raced through my exhausted mind. Just retelling this is triggering my anxiety and PTSD. At the ER, they put me in a private room. I remember vomiting, lying on a bed surrounded by four or five people. I'm not usually one to scream in pain, but I couldn't help it. It was humiliating. They worked to find ways to ease my suffering. Eventually, I was moved to a shared room for the night, waiting for the catheterization lab in the morning.

Before the cath procedure, I requested medication to relax me. It knocked me out cold. I woke up in a private room with a doctor explaining I needed an urgent heart transplant—mine was failing. In my post-sedation haze, I told him I had weekend plans and would come back Monday. He gave me a perplexed look. "You're not going to be able to leave, you'll have to wait for a heart here." That's when I noticed the tube protruding from my neck and the mass of wires around me. Since I was on sedation meds for the cath test, I hadn't fully come in to my senses. I could only focus on not missing out on my future.

Admitted and unable to leave due to my unstable heart, there were COVID-19 isolation restrictions at the hospital. My good friend Jack visited and brought food. The hospital made an exception to the no-visitors rule since I was a "special case"—meaning I might not make it. Jack brought my trusty prepacked hospital bag filled with essentials to make my stay more bearable. I fancy myself a professional hospital resident. If there were an Oscar for Best Hospital Guest, I'd be the award winner. Our visit was brief though, as another wave of pain hit. It was harder to hide my discomfort with someone around. Jack's presence had been a welcomed distraction as I hadn't taken the time to process what was actually happening.

"How long until I get a heart?" I asked the doctor. He said it could take months, but the hospital was where I needed to be. As my condition deteriorated, I'd move up on the waitlist. Then, just one day into my stay, I received stunning news—they had a heart for me. My first thought: Who died to make this possible?

A tangle of emotions washed over me—immense gratitude mixed with fear and guilt that gaining this heart meant someone else lost their life. It finally sank in—this was happening. I called my dad and he booked a flight from Taiwan. In peak pandemic, he was the sole passenger. I wouldn't remember our next conversation. My dad is my go-to person for any life dilemma, always just a call or text away. He'd remind me how pointless it was to agonize over what-ifs. This time, he said this outcome had been expected all along and there was no sense in freaking out. After we hung up, I felt at ease, enough to watch a horror flick on Netflix and drift off to a restful sleep. Scary movies are my go-to comfort films.

I embraced the positivity and prayers pouring in from loved ones near and far. So many people, friends and long-lost acquaintances, responded with an outpouring of love, support, and positive energy.

It was time to surrender control and trust in the expertise of the doctors and surgeons. The night of my surgery, I made sure my long hair was braided and secured in a bun. Experience had taught me this would spare me a tangled mess when I woke up. I felt surprisingly calm. There were two potential outcomes—I'd either wake up with a new heart or not wake up at all. Yup, it was that simple. Why waste energy worrying about the uncontrollable? Still, knowing my dad was on his way to be with me, I prayed for a successful surgery. For his sake more than mine. I'd already put him through enough. And I wasn't done living just yet.

I did wonder about the donor's family though, mourning the loss of their loved one as their heart made its way to me. Would getting a new heart change my personality somehow? What would become of my heart—tossed out as medical waste? The doctor informed me I'd be taken to the OR and might have to wait an hour for my surgeon, Dr. W, to inspect and approve the donor heart. I requested a little "cocktail" to relax me during that time. They agreed.

In the operating room, hooked up to IVs, they gave me the sedative "cocktail." I must have drifted off because next thing I knew, I was waking up extremely uncomfortable due to a breathing tube down my throat. I couldn't move or talk. I think the doctors were telling me I was out of surgery and not to speak. They handed me a pen and paper. As I lay in bed with my eyes closed, I scribbled "this makes me feel like throwing up." Amazingly, they deciphered my handwriting.

The second time I awoke, the breathing tube was gone. The nurses woke me saying I had a phone call—my closest girlfriends were on a group call. I could hear their excitement, all talking over each other. I felt so loved, but completely depleted of energy. I managed to whisper "I'm tired, going to sleep now," before passing out again. Strangely, the pain wasn't as bad as I'd anticipated, at least compared to other discomfort I'd experienced. What struck me first was the thunderous drumming in my ears, like monkeys pounding the walls of my chest cavity. It was so loud, so foreign. This heart was incredibly strong and definitely not my own. I couldn't stop wondering over whose heart now beat within me. The pounding eventually faded hours then days later. Time lost all meaning those first few days in the ICU. It was also my introduction to "the devil's drug," aka Prednisone. Apparently I stayed awake for four days straight.

Emerging from transplant surgery was a profoundly disorienting experience, made even more surreal by the feel and sound of my adopted heart hammering away, a functioning reminder that a piece of someone else was now a major part of my existence. Adapting to a totally different heart rhythm was a jarring process, both physically and psychologically. I essentially had to relearn how to inhale and exhale, how to move my body in tandem with this new pulse.

The post-op delirium was sparked by the sleeplessness and the evil side effects of medications. It was my first ever ICU delirium, which I didn't know was a thing, until I heard other transplant patients' stories. I would love to hear yours, please share if you have one. I've heard some crazy stories, such as a patient who thought everyone in the room was a robot. My story caused me to start unplugging wires from my body, oops! I was seeing my friend in the room partying with me. I remember a nurse rushing into the room to stop me from unplugging everything. I was standing and out of my bed. I pointed to a chair in the room and explained to the nurse that my friend was asleep over there. Our party was over and I was going to go home. The nurse was scared because I was pointing to an empty chair. She asked me if I knew where I was and what had happened to me. She told me I had a heart transplant and I was in the hospital. After reconnecting me to all my monitors and pumps, the nurse administered some heavy-duty medications to knock me out. Finally after four days of being awake, I was able to sleep soundly. When I woke up, all was back to normal. The morning nurse informed me of how I scared my night nurse. I apologized, but at the same time I thought it was quite funny. It felt like someone telling you the drunk things you did the night before. Prior to imagining my friends in my room, I remember calling the nurse to tell her that my wires were dancing. I guess that was a sign that my mind was about to take me on a wild ride.

Receiving a new heart at age 40 was a new beginning—a jumping-off point for a challenging but worthwhile journey. I couldn't have made it through without an abundance of luck, good fortune, and positive energy and love from my dad, friends, and a bonded support system. Never underestimate the power of keeping the faith, in whatever form that takes for you. And more often than not, the universe (and God maybe) will conspire to catch you when you close your eyes and leap.

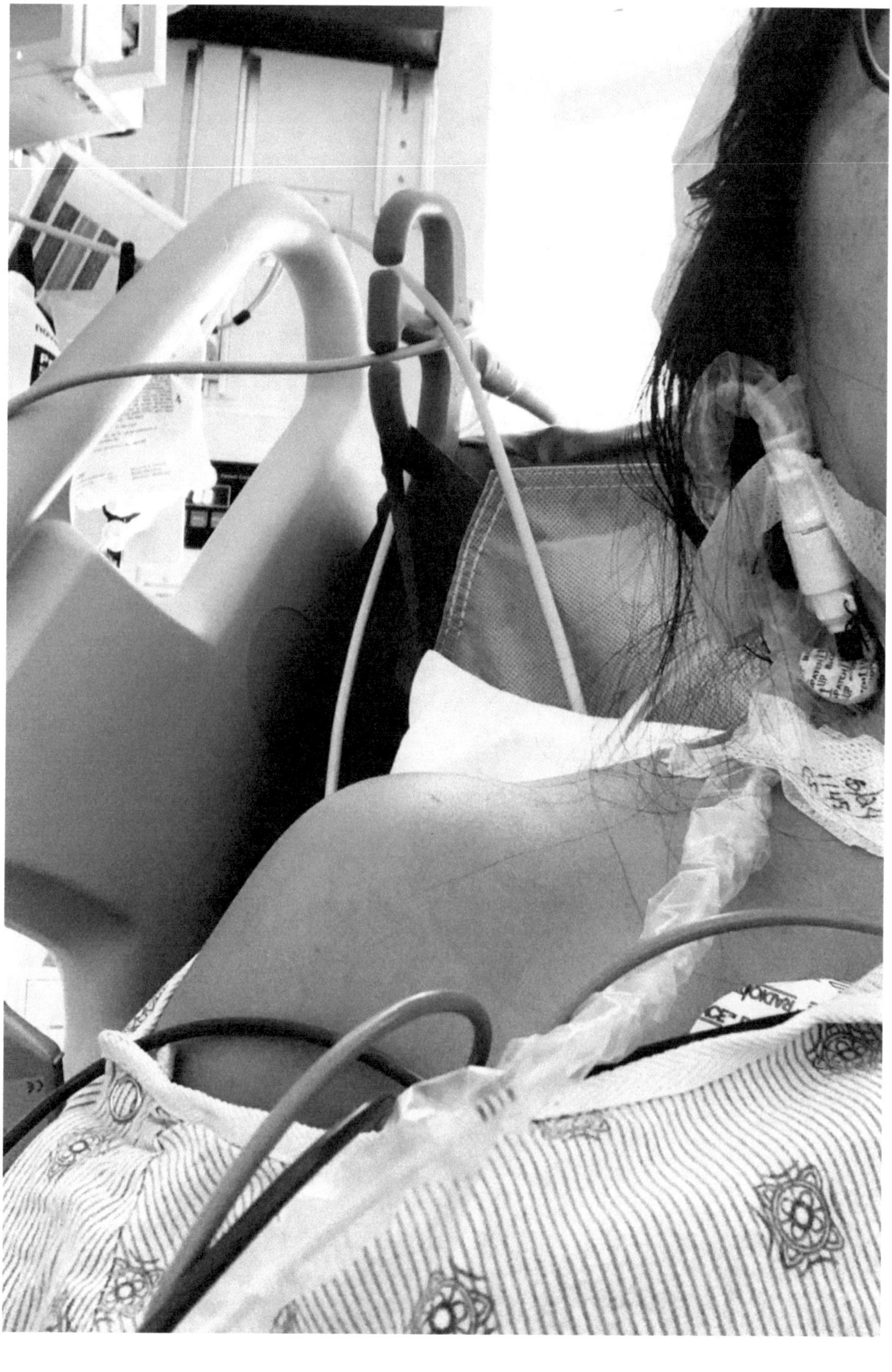

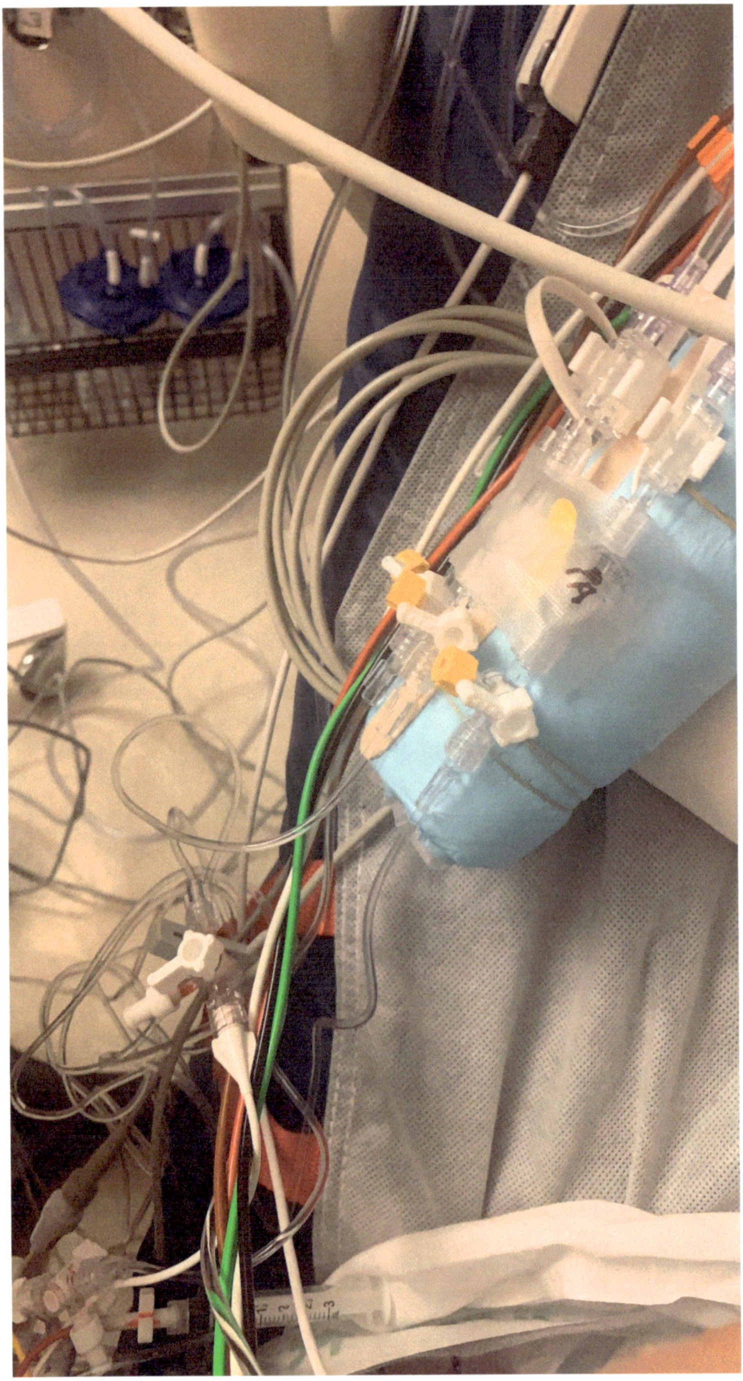

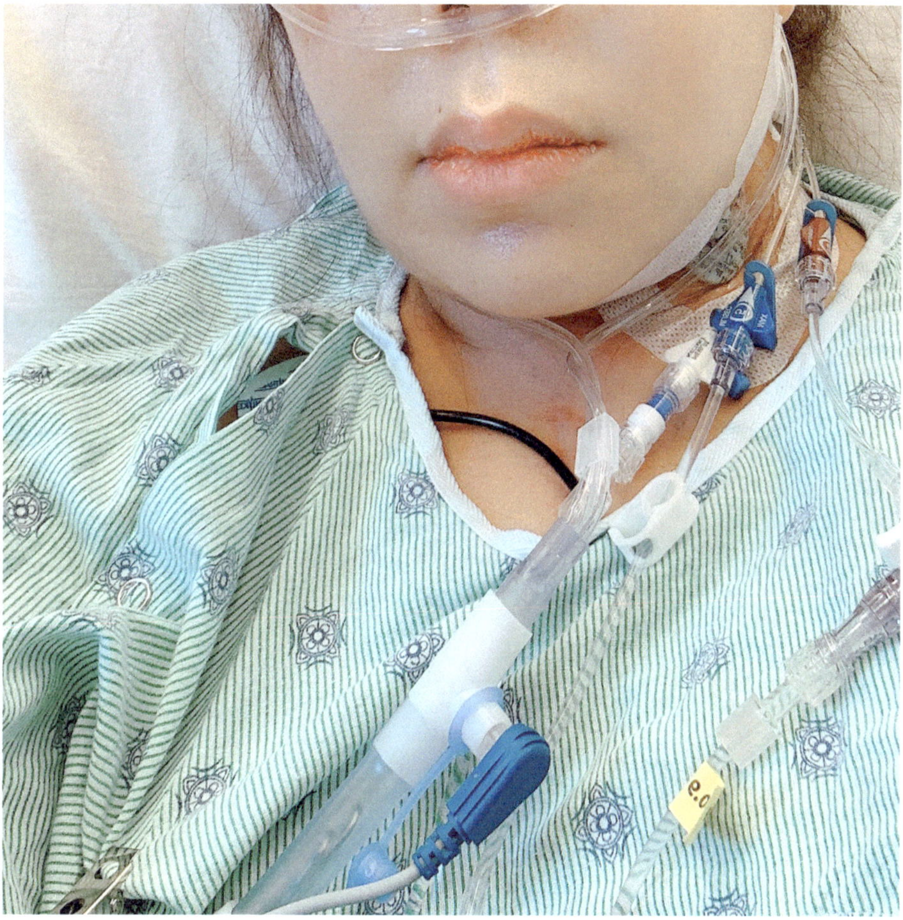

4. THE SUPPORT SYSTEM

"*A little support can go a very long way in someone's life.*" —Unknown

Yo! Can we get a shoutout to all the doctors and nurses? Especially the one who witnessed my ICU delirium. I'd like to personally apologize for scaring her in the middle of the night. It's so crucial to have empathy for nurses during hospital recovery, especially when you've had a transplant at the dawn of a global pandemic and total lockdown. They become your closest allies and caretakers.

I couldn't have asked for a better nursing staff. They went above and beyond, even coming to my room at night to braid my hair so it wouldn't get matted and tangled. For an OCD neat freak like myself, maintaining proper hygiene was a top priority. After washing my hair, they'd carefully braid it and secure it in a tidy bun. Never once did they complain about my high-maintenance requests, always treating me with the utmost kindness, respect, and patience. One nurse even told me I was one of her easiest patients. Granted, she admitted her last patient had hurled the phone at her head. Probably another case of ICU delirium. I was quieter than usual because I don't have anyone I know around me, but the nurses made sure that I felt safe and cared for.

In a COVID-19 world, my dad swooped in on a flight from Taipei to San Francisco, like a knight in hazmat armor—the sole passenger on his flight, dressed head to toe in what looked like a meth cook's getup straight out of an episode of *Breaking Bad.* If you haven't binge-watched that masterpiece of a series yet, I highly recommend it. No time like the present, whether you're waiting for a new heart or laid up recovering from surgery. Truly one of the greatest shows of all time in my opinion. The point is, my dad arrived and I had my number one supporter and champion with me.

My boyfriend at the time also stepped up in a big way, sitting with me for hours on end since I could only have one visitor. He provided invaluable support in the hospital and during those tenuous early days post-transplant. However, in the interest of brevity, I'll keep the story of our involvement as short-lived as his ability to stay faithful. While I'll always be grateful for him showing up when I needed it most, some relationships simply aren't built to withstand life-altering events like an organ transplant. And that's OK. I learned I had to put my own healing and journey first, even if that meant leaving behind partnerships that no longer fit or served me.

Reentry into the real world after an extended hospital stay is never seamless. I had to navigate tricky relationship challenges, like my ex pressuring me to stay in and watch movies 24/7 when all I wanted to do was get out there and experience my new lease on life. When you've stared death in the face and been granted a miraculous second chance, you develop an unquenchable thirst for living that not everyone will understand or share.

Luckily, I had an incredible medical team at UCSF to lean on—the doctors, nurses, and social workers consistently went the extra mile to ensure I felt supported and cared for, well beyond the operating room. When well-meaning loved ones who didn't fully grasp the scope of my situation would suggest I could ease up on my intense medication regimen now that I was "all better." Thankfully, my transplant squad kept me on track, reinforcing how critical it was to stick to the program if I wanted to protect my precious gift and live to enjoy it.

Soon it was time to bust out of my sterile hospital cocoon and head home to finish recovering in my own space. What an incredible feeling to shower in my own bathroom again and sleep in my own bed. I swear, that first night back in my cozy abode, swaddled in my plush, familiar bedding, I felt a rush of gratitude so intense it rivaled any religious epiphany. There really is no place like home.

Even more surreal and exhilarating than a return to my creature comforts was rediscovering what it felt like to draw breath like a normal person. After so many years of gasping for air, I could finally tackle the daunting hills of San Francisco without collapsing in a winded, dizzy heap, fearing I might keel over any second. I remember repeatedly marveling as I inhaled deeply, "OMG! THIS is what oxygen is supposed to feel like! So THIS is how the other half lives!" Simple pleasures I'd taken for granted before, like a functioning set of lungs, now seemed like such a luxury, one I would never waste or fail to appreciate again.

Having an irritated vagus nerve is something they didn't tell me about. It is a weird feeling wanting to stand up from the couch and your body won't do it. I had to think extremely hard when telling my body to stand up. I think it took around 40 seconds for my mind and body to make that connection. A little advice, thinking harder won't make it any faster. This is something that your body will learn and which becomes irrelevant later.

The first few months of being on Prednisone—the devil's drug—will make you restless, you will have a lot of energy to do things. I hiked the first weekend that I was out of the hospital, and I never hiked, so it was wild! I have also developed PTSD for water. After the transplant, I failed the swallowing test twice, so I was not allowed to drink water on my own for about three days. The pain of thirst is worse than a transplant because it is a struggle of waiting. Waiting on taking that first sip of water. I can imagine this is what it feels like when a person is dying of thirst in a desert. I now own about 100 different types of water bottle that can be found in my car, purse, bedroom, living room, and sometimes bathroom.

After going radio silent on social media during the whirlwind of my surgery and immediate recovery, I finally logged back onto Facebook, stunned and moved to discover thousands upon thousands of messages, comments, and prayers from people near and far. I was overwhelmed in the best, most humbling way as I scrolled through this deluge of love, encouragement, and solidarity. Some well-wishes came from old childhood friends I hadn't spoken to in decades. Family, friends, acquaintances, coworkers past and present—my whole extended network had rallied behind me, sharing messages of strength and hope. It was like the world's biggest, most jubilant digital group hug. I felt fortunate beyond measure to realize just how expansive and engaged my circle was, and how many lives I'd touched who were now reciprocating that impact tenfold. So thanks for that nudge to reconnect, Zuck! What would us transplant patients do without this modern marvel of human connection that the brilliant minds at Facebook have gifted us? Besides safeguard our fragile democracies and attention spans, of course.

Joking aside, one virtual community in particular became a lifeline for me—a Facebook group called "Heart Transplant Support" filled with fellow survivors, warriors, and zipper-club members trading battle stories, comparing scars, and generously pouring out information and resources. If only I'd known this treasure trove existed back when I was being wheeled in for my surgery! It would have answered so many burning questions and eased so much of my confusion and fear.

I also stumbled upon a posse of badass lady heart-havers on Instagram who organized regular Zoom hangs during lockdown. As a surgery newbie still getting my sea legs under me, these women from across the globe swooped in like the cavalry to talk me through every doubt, obstacle, and head-scratcher. This tight-knit crew, captained by a sassy Brit who'd been navigating the transplant waters since adolescence met my every "is this normal?!" freakout with wisdom, empathy, and desperately needed belly laughs. I marveled at how this woman had weathered all the gnarly medication side effects since her teen years—what strength of character that must have taken! She was a walking master class in rolling with the punches.

I also linked up with a gal closer to home, just an hour's drive away, who'd started a nonprofit dubbed the Heartfelt Help Foundation. Genius in its simplicity, this organization assists transplant patients in securing affordable housing close to their hospital for the duration of treatment and monitoring. An absolutely brilliant concept to ease some of the logistical and financial strain of this intense process, especially for cash-strapped families desperate to stay near their beloveds. We're all in this together, and I'm a big believer in lifting as we climb. So when an opportunity presents itself to lighten the load of a fellow zipper-club member, I say strap on your tool belt and get to work!

Oh, did I not explain that lingo yet? See, we heart transplant recipients affectionately refer to our clan as the "zipper club," a nod to the striking chest scars we sport from collarbone to ribcage. These vivid souvenirs, resembling an off-center zipper pull, serve as our membership badges—visible reminders of the physical, mental, and emotional mountains we've scaled together. This unique club brims with some of the most resilient, hopeful, and flat-out inspiring folks you'll ever have the honor of knowing. After all, you can't cheat death without developing some seriously superhuman tenacity and spunk.

I've become a vocal advocate for building and plugging into support networks, having experienced firsthand how powerfully this connection buoys health outcomes and overall quality of life. Whether newly diagnosed or years out from a successful transplant, surrounding yourself with people who intimately "get" your reality and can relate on a cellular level (literally!) is nourishing on so many levels.

I've had the privilege of guiding several pre-transplant patients through their own journeys, paying forward the invaluable coaching and cheerleading I received when I was the new kid on the block. One gentleman, Bob, reached out during his anxious waiting period for a donor match. Cut to a year later, when he sent me the most beautiful, tear-jerking note on my transplant anniversary, remembering the exact date and honoring how far we'd both come. Another dear heart, a young man from Thailand, made sure to drop me a line the minute he regained consciousness after his big surgery. Providing even a tiny sliver of clarity or comfort to these courageous souls as they embark on the ride of their lives, as others did for me, has been immensely healing and rewarding.

I can't emphasize enough how vital community is when it comes to thriving, not just surviving, with a chronic condition like heart failure or organ rejection. Your support squad can take infinitely diverse forms—family, medical staff, fellow transplantees, faith groups, four-legged companions, you name it! Heck, my life raft through choppy emotional waters came in the pint-sized package of a goofy fluffball I like to call my "unofficial therapy dog." You heard me right. Sometimes the MVP on your team wears a furry coat and sports a wagging tail.

Allow me to introduce you to Benedict Le Petit (Beni), the short-legged, 23-pound Cavalier-Bichon mix who's been my constant shadow, cuddle buddy, and emotional support animal from the day I broke free from the ICU. Beni was actually my transplant present from my dad. On the inevitable tough days, this little guy freely gives me his unconditional adoration, playful spirit, and knack for making me laugh until I've forgotten whatever was stressing me out minutes before. When I'm getting too deep into my head, spiraling about this weird new heart flutter or that suspicious looking mole, one glance at Beni yanks me out of the anxiety whirlpool. Prior to receiving Beni, I had another canine companion, Mr. Cheese. He was a Chihuahua who had been with me pre-transplant and lived to be 19 years old. Mr. Cheese was very important and special to me as well. A quick snuggle or belly-rub session with my fluffy besties, and suddenly the world seems less scary and overwhelming. Never underestimate the therapeutic power of devoted furry friends!

Early into my recovery, I had to confront some sneaky medical PTSD. Out of nowhere, my pulse would spike and my brain would instantly jump to worst-case scenarios. "Is this the beginning of rejection? Am I in full-blown organ failure again?!" Usually it was just good old-fashioned panic, a souvenir of the trauma my body and mind had endured.

With the help of a fantastic therapist specializing in chronic illness and an arsenal of holistic coping tools like meditation and breathwork, I slowly learned to climb out of crisis mode and manage my stress response. Retraining my nervous system to distinguish between false alarms and legitimate red flags was a crucial step in reclaiming my peace and equilibrium.

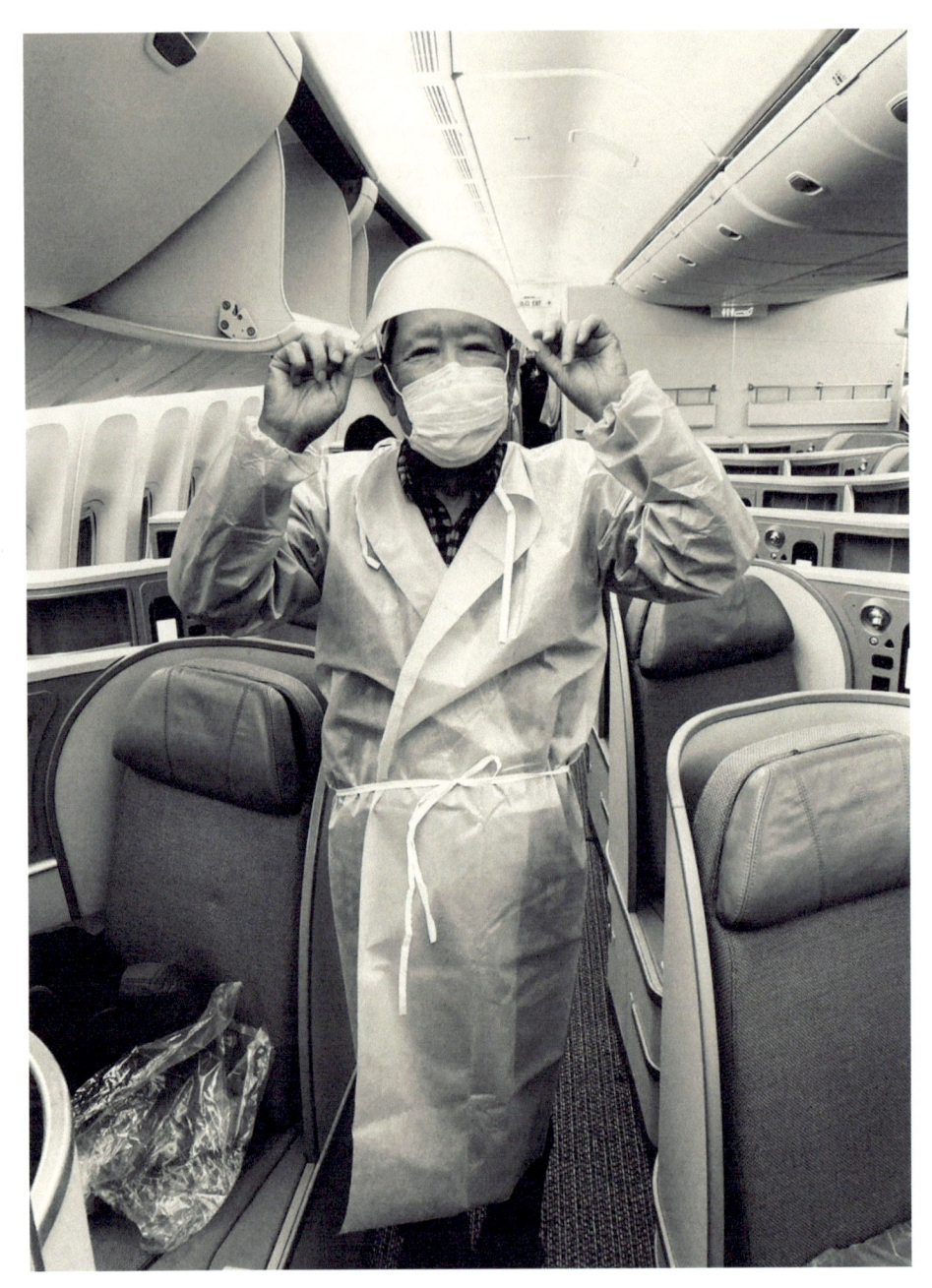

the solo passenger

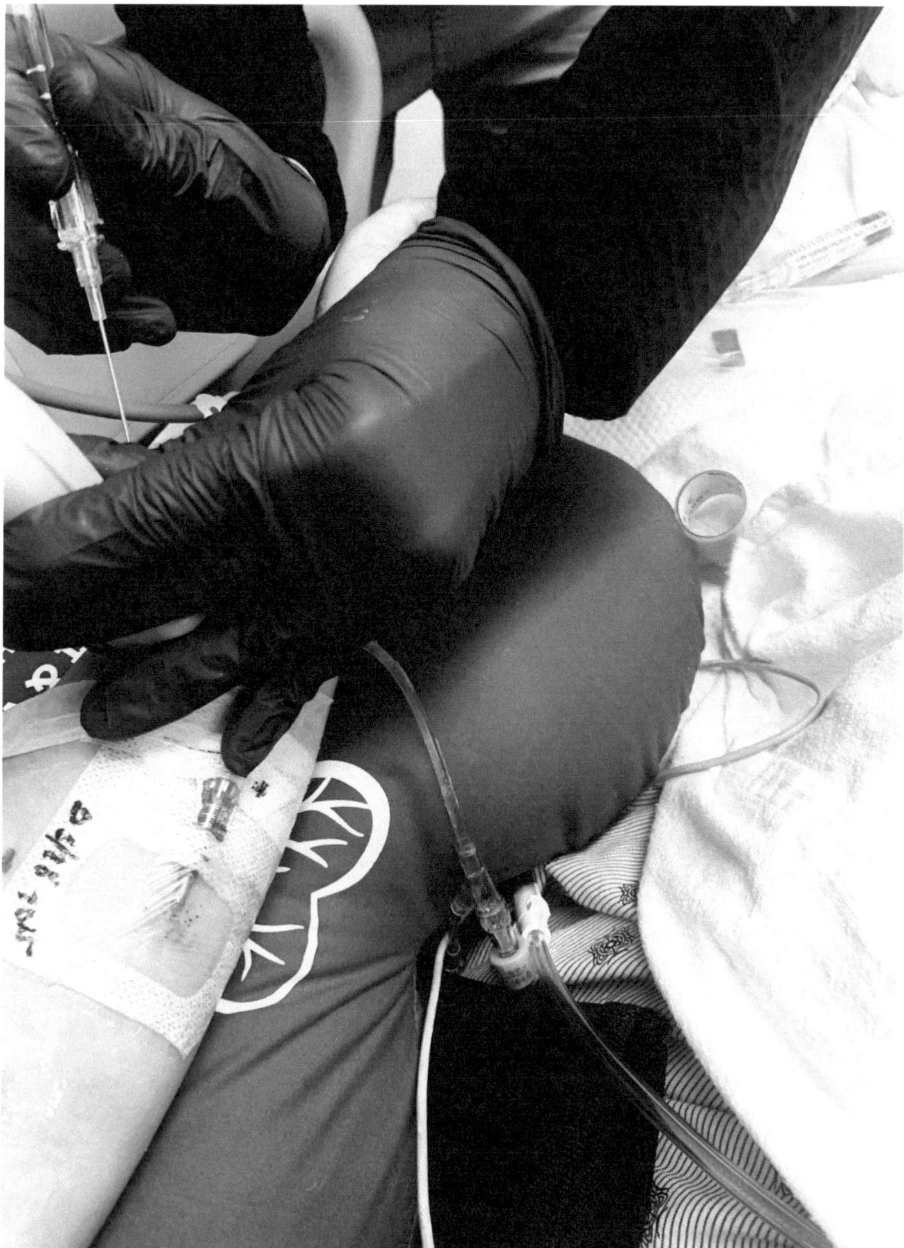

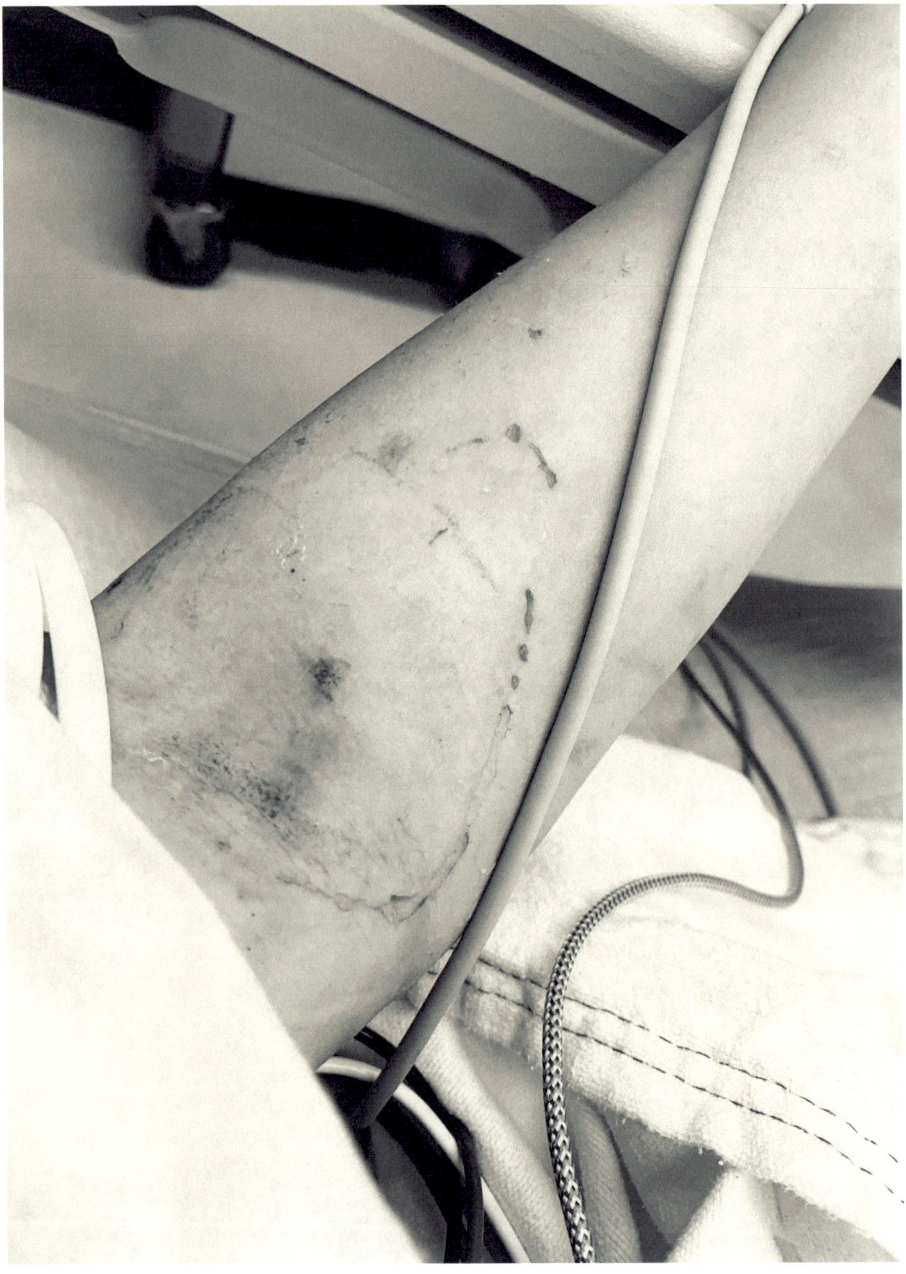

my support system

Special Chapter

5. FYI

"*What people don't tell you, so I will.*"— Nerrisa Lu

When you're facing a heart transplant, there's a wealth of information that your medical team will share with you. They'll brief you on the surgery, the immediate recovery process, and the medications you'll need to take. However, there's a whole world of practical, day-to-day experiences that often go unmentioned. These are the little things that can make a big difference in your life as a transplant recipient, the nuggets of wisdom you typically only learn from fellow zipper-club members or through your own trial and error.

That's why connecting with other transplant patients and joining support groups is so crucial—it's like getting the inside scoop on this wild journey we're all navigating together. As a recovering heart transplant patient myself, I've learned a thing or two about what to expect, and I'm here to share some handy tips that your transplant team might not tell you. First and foremost, let's talk about the importance of having a bag ready for ER trips. Trust me on this one—I know from experience that every time I go into an emergency room, I could end up staying for days. It's far better to be prepared than to be caught off guard. So, what should you pack in this magical bag of preparedness? Let me break it down for you:

A robe: You know those hospital gowns are going to be showing your booty, and you don't want the whole world to see it. Plus, a robe will keep your back warm during those chilly hospital nights. Phone charger with an extension cord: This is arguably the most important item in your bag. Hospital-room layouts are rarely designed with patient convenience in mind, and you'll quickly discover that the electrical outlets are frustratingly far from your bed. A long extension cord will be your lifeline, allowing you to keep your phone charged and within reach. After all, how else are you going to update your Instagram, Facebook, X (formerly Twitter), or whatever social media platform is trendy by the time you're reading this? Pajama pants or shorts: Again, this is all about covering up your booty and maintaining some normalcy in the hospital environment. Hair tie, hairbrush, toothbrush, face wash, face cream: Basically, pack as if you're going on vacation. Maintaining your usual grooming routines can help you feel more like yourself in the sterile hospital environment. Tablet or laptop: Download all your favorite shows ahead of time. Personally, I like to watch horror movies during my hospital stays. It might sound weird, but I find it helps with my anxiety. After all, it's better to be scared by a movie than by the real-life situations going on around you.

HEART TO HEART

Now, let me give you a more detailed rundown of what goes into Nerrisa's hospital bag. Consider this your ultimate packing list:

Electronics: We're part robot now, right? Might as well embrace it. Make sure you have your phone, tablet, laptop—whatever devices you rely on to stay connected and entertained. Long extension cord: I can't stress this enough. The wall plug is never going to reach your bed, and there will be times when you can't get out of bed without getting tangled in the billions of wires attached to your body. You'll be thanking me when you can comfortably scroll through TikTok without your arm going numb from reaching for your charger. Noise-canceling headphones: Unless you enjoy the 24/7 symphony of beeping machines while you sleep (spoiler alert: you won't), these will be a godsend. They might not give you a full night's rest, but they'll at least grant you a few hours of peace before the next blood draw. Pajama bottoms: I know I mentioned this before, but it bears repeating. Hospital gowns are not known for their modesty. Pajama bottoms will keep you covered and warm. Throw blanket: Treat yourself to something soft and comfy from Amazon. Hospital bedding leaves a lot to be desired in the comfort department. If you're going to be there for a while (and let's face it, you probably will be), you might as well be as cozy as possible. Pro tip: bringing your own pillow is a game-changer too. Comfy slippers or a robe: Why not both? Anything that makes you feel more at home in the clinical hospital environment is a win. Your daily beauty routine essentials: Listen, just because you're in the hospital, doesn't mean you have to let your skincare game slip. Bring your eye cream, face masks, face wash, lotion, nail clippers, tweezers—whatever makes you feel human. Not only will it help you maintain some normalcy, but it's also a great way to kill time between nurse check-ins. A good book: During my recovery, I read *Where the Crawdads Sing*. It was fantastic and a great distraction from hospital life. Pack whatever genre speaks to you—mystery, romance, science fiction, or maybe even a book about heart health (though you might be a bit sick of that topic by now). I'm happy to report that this bag has been officially retired as of one year post-transplant. I'm no longer a frequent flyer at the hospital, which is definitely something to celebrate!

Now, let's dive into some of the things they don't tell you about life after transplant surgery. These are the tidbits of information I wish someone had shared with me beforehand:

Filling your pill box is going to become your second job. Don't panic—it gets easier after you do it for the 100th time. In the beginning, you'll be taking so many medications that you'll wonder how on earth you're going to remember all these names. But trust me, before long, you'll be rattling off drug names like a seasoned pharmacist. "Cocktails" are your new best friend during autopsies and cath labs. Always, and I mean always, tell your doctor you'd like the "feel-good cocktail" during your tests. And no, I'm not talking about a martini (though that would be nice). I'm referring to the combination of drugs they can give you to make these procedures more comfortable. Don't be shy about asking for it—your comfort matters. Say goodbye to some of your favorite foods. No more sushi, medium-rare steaks, fresh oysters, grapefruit, and my personal favorite, dragon fruit. If you're reading this before your transplant, I suggest you hit up Uber Eats right now and indulge in these treats one last time. I particularly miss uni (sea urchin)—it's been years, and I still dream about it sometimes. And if your go-to drink at the bar was a greyhound (vodka and grapefruit juice), I'm sorry to say you'll need to find a new signature cocktail. Gardening is off-limits, at least for the first year. I learned this the hard way by getting an infection in my first year post-transplant. DO NOT TRY THIS! I know it might seem harmless, but the bacteria in soil can be dangerous for immunosuppressed transplant recipients. Your new heart is precious—don't risk it for a tomato plant. You can keep your pets! This is not negotiable, so don't let anyone tell you otherwise. Your fur babies are family, and they can stay. However, for the first year post-transplant, have someone else clean up their poop. It's just safer that way. Prepare yourself for infusion-center visits. You'll be getting infusions for the first few months post-transplant, and you'll likely be in the same area as cancer patients. It can be emotionally challenging to see others going through their own health battles. It's OK to feel sad or overwhelmed—just remember that you're all warriors in your own way. Brace yourself for some temporary side effects from the medications. You might develop temporary diabetes, lose bone density, or experience hair loss. I know, it sounds scary. But remember the key word here: temporary. These side effects usually improve as your medication doses are adjusted over time. On a positive note, you'll enjoy everything so much more. Your bed will feel more comfortable, food will taste better, the air will seem fresher. You'll become the person who gives less of a damn about small things. There's something incredibly freeing about getting a second chance at life—it puts everything into perspective. One of the most important things I've learned on this journey is the value of connecting with other transplant recipients. That's why I highly recommend following Transplant Helper by Jim Murrell on YouTube (@transplanthelper). Jim provides invaluable insights and tips for navigating life post-transplant, and his channel is a great resource for both patients and their families.

Remember, while the medical aspects of your transplant journey are crucial, it's often these practical, day-to-day tips that can make your life easier and more comfortable. Don't be afraid to reach out to other transplant recipients or join support groups—the transplant community is incredibly supportive and always ready to share their wisdom.

yes your hair will fall out (right) but it will also grow back fuller (left)

Live everyday like it's the first day of your life

6. ABOUT RECOVERY

"*Live every day like it's the FIRST day of your life.*"—Unknown

The moment I woke up after my heart transplant surgery, I took a deep breath and realized this was a day I might not have been able to experience. Today is an extra day of life. Whatever happens, I will embrace it, good or bad, it is a bonus. The easiest thing I could compare it to was like playing the video game Super Mario Bros. For any gamers out there, you know that feeling when you're about to fall into a pit yet you snag an extra-life mushroom? That surge of excitement, relief, and renewed determination because you cheated death and got an extra life and defeated the game. That's exactly how I felt waking up with my new heart. Every moment from that point forward was a bonus and a chance for me to finish things. If I were Mario, Beni would definitely be my Yoshi.

My doctor had cautioned me to enjoy life but with care, reminding me that my treatment plan was different from what it had been. It was impossible for me to predict how much everything would be different from this moment on. But beyond the doctor's medical suggestions, a question loomed large in my mind: *what do I do now?* Continuing life as it was before the transplant seemed impossible. How could it be the same when everything would be so much better now? Every experience from this moment on was a gift, bestowed upon me by another human's incredible generosity. It was a trippy thought, to say the least. As usual, life had a way of surprising me with unexpected joys and connections. One of my biggest decisions was to reach out to my donor's family. Typically, it's recommended that you wait awhile before trying to contact your donor's family. But I felt driven to find out who my donor was.

After much internal debate mixed with nervousness, I decided to send a Christmas card to my donor's family. I wanted to express my immense gratitude and share a bit about the life (my life) their loved one's heart was now supporting. I agonized over every word, wondering how they might receive it. Would it bring them comfort or be a painful reminder of their loved one who died?

It was also the first holiday her family would be spending without her. At the time I didn't even know if it was a "her" or "him." I just knew it was the first holiday without their loved one and that must be difficult. I knew not to expect a letter in return, because every family deals with death differently. This heart that I feel daily is foreign and I can't help but think, *will I ever know who's heart is in my body?* When I dropped that card in the mail, I had no idea of the beautiful journey it would set in motion. It didn't take long before I was surprised to receive a response from my donor's mom. The next letter I received was a letter from the donor network, my donor's mom had signed a form to release her information to me. I had her phone number in my hand. I was filled with anxiety and emotion all at once. I did not waste a second before unlocking my phone, entering her number and typing the first text message then pressing "send." I was so nervous and hoped that I wasn't being too insensitive and intrusive.

She shared photos and stories about her daughter, Bre, and suddenly my donor became real—she was a young woman in her 20s with a life, dreams, and a family who loved her deeply.

We began to exchange letters and texts, slowly getting to know each other and building a relationship I never could have anticipated. I replied with a letter and a picture of my 41st birthday. I told her about myself and wanted to share that this birthday would not have happened without my gift.

My connection to my donor and her family is so much stronger than I ever could have expected. I felt so lucky because I've only seen these types of scenarios in movies. I did not know it could be so real. It blossomed into a beautiful connection and gave me a sense of an extended family I never could have imagined. I was super excited and emotional to receive the letters and to learn that my donor came from a huge family who loved her so much. Not that it should matter, but I am glad I have a heart of a good person.

I discovered that Bre's mom, Jen, was only two years older than me. This unexpected similarity made our connection feel even more special and unlikely. It was as if the universe had aligned in the most incredible way to bring us together.

HEART TO HEART

When we finally decided to meet in person, I was a bundle of nerves. What if she didn't like me? Should I drink in front of her? These questions plagued me as I waited for her to arrive. We had planned to meet for margaritas, and I found myself wondering if it was appropriate to drink alcohol in front of the mother of my heart donor. Would she think I wasn't taking good care of Bre's heart?

But all my worries melted away the moment I saw Jen. The emotion on her face when she first laid eyes on me is something I'll never forget. It was a complex mix of joy, sorrow, and wonder. For me, seeing her was like looking at a piece of Bre—I could never imagine what it is like to lose a child, but in that moment, I could feel it when she hugged me tight. Jen gives the best hugs.

That day, we drank margaritas (turns out Jen can drink me under the table!), laughed, cried, and shared stories. She brought me gifts—little mementos of Bre's life that I now treasure. One of the most touching was a Christmas ornament with Bre's picture on it. It now hangs on my tree every year, a reminder of the incredible gift I've been given.

As we spent time together, Bre's extended family embraced me with open arms. They cried tears of joy and heartache at our first meeting, telling me stories about Bre and marveling at the way life had brought us together. I began to feel like an honorary member of their family, receiving birthday cards and exchanging regular updates about our lives. Mama Jen and I talk a few days a week. She is now a big part of my life. I not only received a heart from Bre, she also gave me an extra person to love.

To honor Bre and carry her with me always, I decided to get a tattoo. It's her nickname, "Bre Bird," inked on my skin as a permanent reminder of the life that lives on in me. Every time I see it, I'm filled with gratitude and a renewed commitment to live this bonus life to its fullest.

However, amid all the cheerfulness of this new connection, I had a nagging worry of survivor's guilt. Is it OK that I never got the meaning of it? Perhaps I never felt survivor's guilt or don't fully understand it? When I Googled what survivor's guilt is, Google said it is how patients often feel guilty about benefiting from the donor's death. I never considered that I am benefiting from someone's death. In fact, the sound of that makes me feel uncomfortable. "Benefiting" from someone sounds like you are "using" them. I am not benefiting from my donor, rather, I feel that we are living on together as one. I am carrying a piece of Bri with me on my journey. With the time she has given me, together we can make the world better. I know that sounds cheesy, but remember the promise that I made to God when I wasn't even sure if I was religious? Well, apparently a higher power out there believes that I deserve this second chance, and I better fulfill my promise.

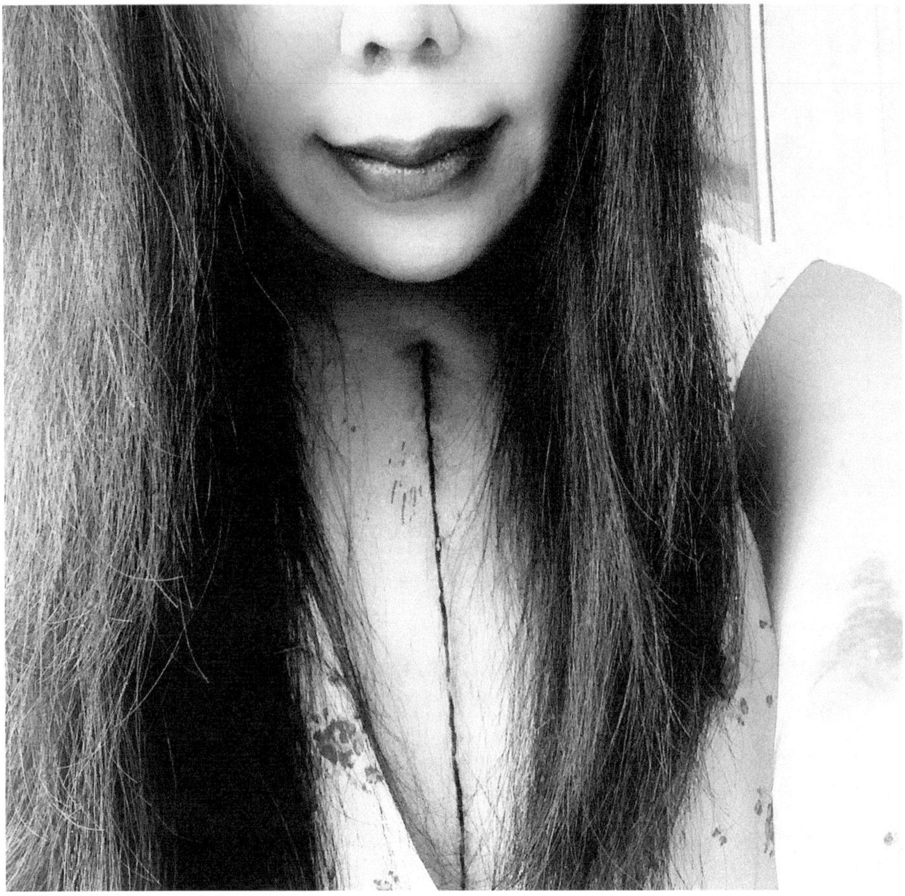

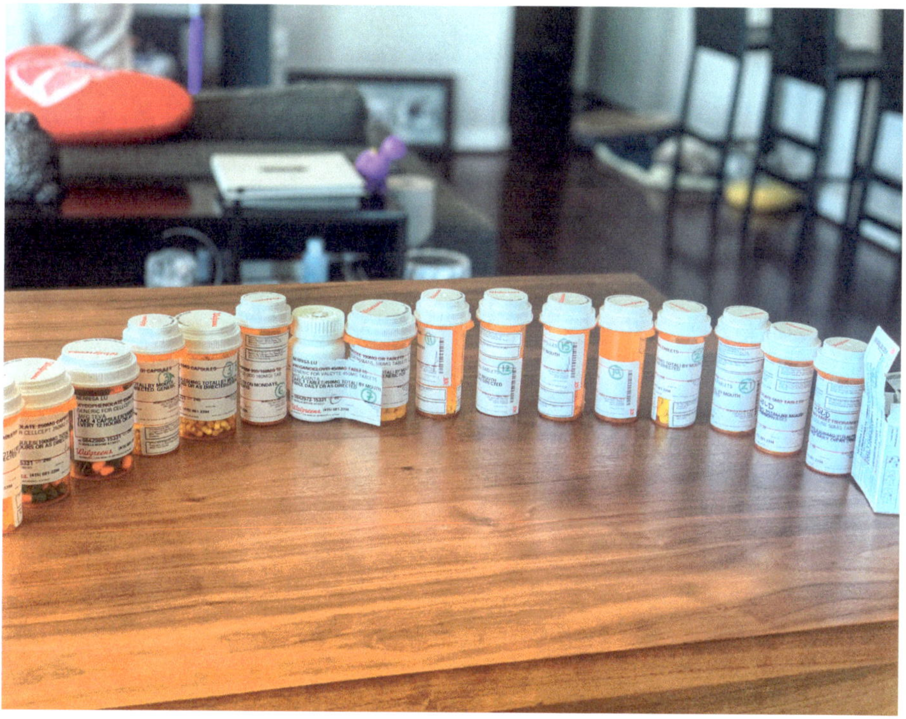

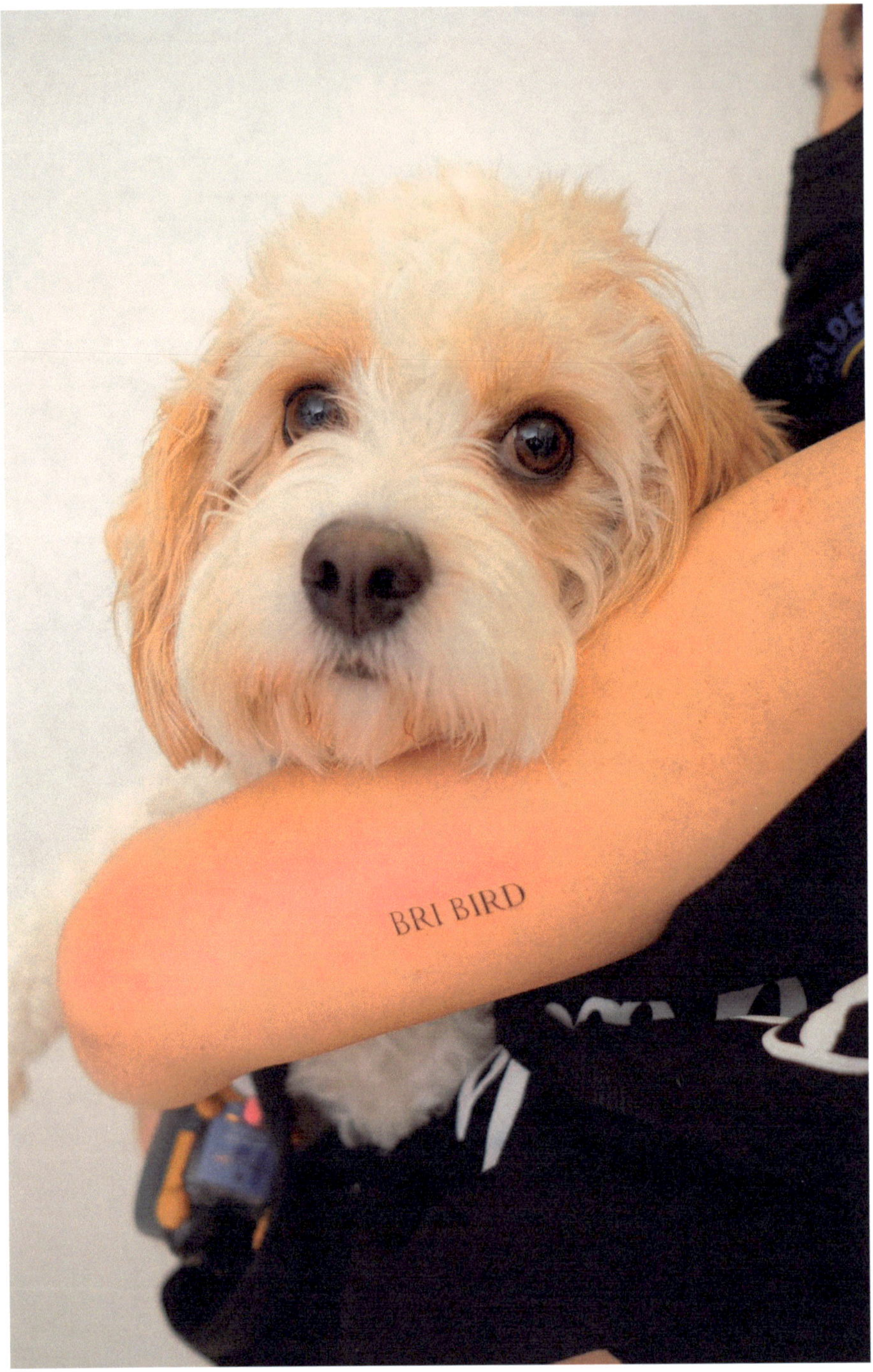
BRI BIRD

7. WHAT NOW?

"Just because we carry it well, doesn't mean it is not heavy." —Unknown

Life after a heart transplant is complicated, filled with ups and downs. While the world may see you as a miraculous recovery, those of us who've walked this path know that the weight we carry is often invisible to others. This chapter is about the struggles after transplant—the pros and cons, the visible and invisible battles we face every day.

Let's start with something positive—our scars. That long line down our chest, affectionately known as the "zipper," is more than just a surgical scar. It's a badge of honor, a mark of membership in an exclusive club, and quite possibly the coolest battle scar you've ever seen.

When I was finally healed enough, I couldn't wait to show off my zipper scar. It felt like a visual representation of everything I'd been through, a testament to my survival.

There's something empowering about having a visible sign of your journey. No longer do I have to explain why I can't do certain things—people can see the evidence of my struggle right there on my chest.

Connecting with other transplant patients who also sport the zipper scar has been an incredible experience. We understand each other on a deeper level, bonded by our shared experiences and the visible reminder we carry with us always. Being a member of the "zipper club" has some unexpected perks. I've found that people often give me special treatment when they see it. It's like having a VIP badge permanently attached to my chest. While I never want to take advantage of this, I can't deny that it's sometimes nice to be treated with extra care and consideration.

Joking or not joking aside, we do have a very sexy battle wound. It builds character, makes us look strong, and it just made our life that much more interesting to other people. Whatever mediocre life you had before is gone. Your story will forever be the kind where people gasp when they listen.

You see, with this scar, we no longer have to explain in great detail why we can't do certain things. People will just assume we can't do certain things, which makes it very convenient. And because of the simple things that we can do now, people will think we are an inspiration. Which we ARE, of course, but it is not like we have another option. We are just living in our own way.

It's not that we don't suffer anymore, we still do. But we've graduated to a visible disability! You belong to this special club where you don't have to feel alone because I am also one of the members. That is why I am sharing my story, because I am wondering if people out there also can relate to me. Sharing my story helps make the load that I carry less heavy. I suggest you share your story too, and if you are unable to, I hope I can be the voice for you.

Through this heart transplant journey, I've discovered a new purpose—to spread hope, strength, and positivity to others facing similar challenges. By sharing my story and the lessons I've learned, I hope to inspire and empower fellow heart warriors to embrace life fully, despite its challenges.

8. YOUR HOMEWORK

What's a self-help book without a little homework, right? Don't worry, I promise this won't feel like those dreaded high-school assignments. Instead, think of it as a gift to yourself—a way to capture the good moments, reflect on your journey, and set intentions for the future.

Here's the assignment I'm giving you. You can use these last few pages to start, but I highly recommend investing in a beautiful journal to continue this practice. Trust me, there's something special about putting pen to paper in a book that feels good in your hands.

Every day, I want you to answer these four questions:

How do you feel physically/mentally today? What is something good that happened today? What did you contribute to making the world better today? Perhaps you gave someone a smile? Told someone to have a nice day? Helped open a door? What is something positive you would like to do tomorrow? Now, I know what you're thinking. "Nerrisa, life isn't all sunshine and rainbows. Shitty things happen all the time!" And you're absolutely right. But here's the thing—shitty things will continue to happen whether we focus on them or not. So why not make a conscious effort to write down the good moments and memories?

HEART TO HEART

This exercise isn't about ignoring the tough stuff. It's about training our brains to notice and appreciate the positive aspects of our lives, no matter how small they might seem. It's about recognizing the impact we have on the world around us, even on our hardest days.

Let's take it a step further. I want you to really ponder this question: What would the world miss if you weren't here? It's a heavy question, I know. But think about it—instead of dying, you received a heart transplant and lived. Your very existence from that moment on is changing the world in ways you might not even realize.

To illustrate this point, I suggest you watch a movie called *Sliding Doors*. It's a fantastic film featuring Gwyneth Paltrow that explores two separate scenarios that evolve from a single moment—catching or missing a subway train. It's a powerful demonstration of how one tiny decision can dramatically alter the course of our lives.

This concept is closely related to something called the butterfly effect. Have you heard of it? It's a phenomenon whereby a minimal localized change in a complex system can have large effects elsewhere. In simpler terms, small actions can lead to big changes.

Let me give you an example of the butterfly effect in action. Imagine you're walking down the street and you give a stranger a simple smile. That small act of kindness could turn their bad day into a good one. (Just don't give them a creepy smile—remember, the butterfly effect can go both ways, good and bad. Yikes!) As a result of your smile, that person might carry that positive energy forward, passing it on to others they encounter throughout their day.

Or consider this scenario: you stop to chat with a stranger at a crosswalk while waiting for the light to change. That two-minute conversation might seem insignificant to you, but what if it saved their life? Maybe they were distracted and would have walked into traffic if you hadn't engaged them in conversation. OK, maybe that's an extreme example. But people text and walk all the time! Distractions happen anywhere and everywhere.

The point is, trying out the butterfly effect can demonstrate that there are infinite possibilities in this life. It invites us to consider alternate, parallel, or multi-universes (multiverses) where things might have turned out differently. There are universes out there where you didn't get the heart transplant. But I believe the universe where you lived—this universe—is a better place because you're in it.

So, as you sit down each day to do this homework, I want you to really think about these questions. When you consider how you feel physically and mentally, be honest with yourself. Some days you might feel on top of the world, and other days you might feel like you've been hit by a truck. Both are OK. The important thing is to acknowledge how you're feeling without judgment.

When you think about something good that happened, don't dismiss the small things. Maybe you had a really great cup of coffee this morning. Maybe your favorite song came on the radio. Maybe you got through a tough medical appointment and treated yourself to ice cream afterwards. All of these count as good things.

Reflecting on how you contributed to making the world better might feel challenging at first, especially on days when you're not feeling your best. But remember, even the smallest acts of kindness count. Did you let someone merge in front of you in traffic? Did you compliment a coworker on their work? Did you simply choose to be patient with yourself when you were struggling? These are all ways of making the world a little bit better.

And finally, when you think about something positive you'd like to do tomorrow, don't put pressure on yourself to come up with grand gestures. Maybe you want to call a friend you haven't spoken to in a while. Maybe you want to try a new recipe. Maybe you just want to spend an extra five minutes cuddling with your pet in the morning. The key is to give yourself something to look forward to, no matter how small.

Go grab that beautiful journal, find a cozy spot, and start writing. Your homework begins now, but trust me, this is one assignment you'll actually look forward to completing. Who knows? The simple act of putting pen to paper might just be the butterfly wings that set off a chain reaction of positivity in your life.

And hey, if you're ever feeling stuck or uninspired, just remember: somewhere out there in the multiverse, there's a version of you who didn't get to do this homework. But you? You're here. You're alive. You're making the world a better place, one journal entry at a time. So make it count, heart warrior.

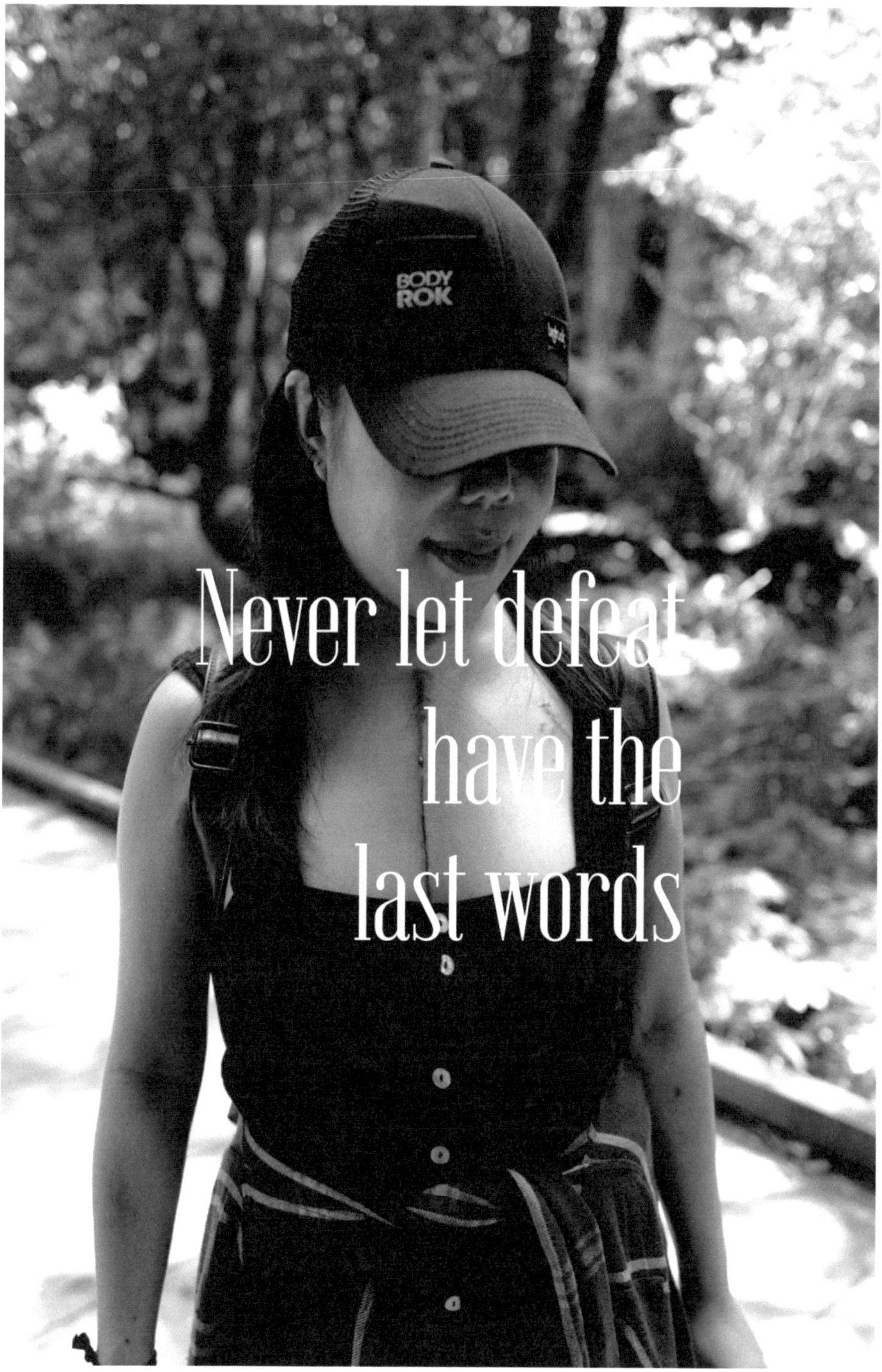
BODY
ROK
Never let defeat
have the
last words

9. MY LAST WORDS

"*Never let defeat have the last words.*"—Unknown

What shall I leave you with? Usually at the end of a self-help book, the author reinforces new habits that they've successfully convinced you to have. After all, I am only sharing my story and one person's point of view on how to deal with life before, during, and after a transplant. This is your second chance at life, you can do whatever you want with it. That's your own choice. I am just here to remind you that not everyone was lucky enough to receive a heart and not everyone survived their surgery. Please don't forget that.

Your life post-transplant is yours to live as you see fit. Make it count, make it meaningful, make it yours. And if you ever find yourself forgetting how far you've come, put your hand on your chest and feel that heartbeat and remember—you're still here, you're still fighting, and you've got one hell of a story to tell.

Your birthdays from now on will have a different meaning. You are aging, think about what a blessing that is. If you don't appreciate this second chance at life, you can go F yourself. Waste it if you want to. But that's definitely not in my playbook. This is my second chance at life and I chose to live it as brilliantly and boldly as I wish. Now, if only I could win the lottery so I can also finance my bold new life.

now you can run but wait for your loved ones

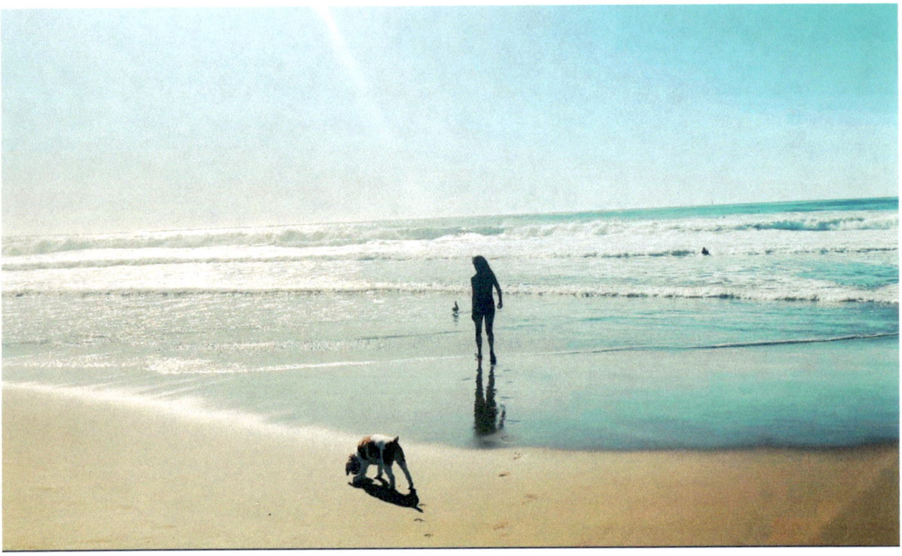

THANK YOU

Doctors are angels in disguise. These are the gifted physicians that appeared in my life, in the order that we met.

Dr. Ruey Sun, Dr. Peter Teng, Dr. Byron Lee, Dr. Liviu Klein, Dr. George Wieselthaler.

I want to thank all my doctors and nurses. Without you, I would be ashes in a fancy bottle.

StoryTerrace

Made in the USA
Columbia, SC
09 February 2025